To: Taggart,

enjoy every poem that
flows your way.

Cardboard Wings

Piper M. L. Bringman

Piper B. (signature)

A Publication of The Poetry Box® Young Artist Series

ISBN: 978-1-948461-27-6
Printed in the United States of America.

Published by The Poetry Box®, 2019
   under the Young Artist Series imprint
Portland, Oregon
ThePoetryBox.com

For my beloved Bunny Cat
You are always in my heart

Contents

The Heart of a Ship

My heart is like a ship's living quarters
A tidy compartment full of simple yet beautiful things
All neatly nailed in place

The lower bunk for my body
The upper for my soul

When everything is in order,
It all runs smoothly over the waves

When a storm hits however,
All the nails come flying out
Twisted and bent like angry words,
And the boat spins figurehead first
Into the pulling tide
Scattering jagged little pieces around the deck

It takes time to fix what is broken
And tidy up the boat
But when the ocean is calm,
Watch for a curious child
Standing tiptoe upon the nailed-down desk
Peeping through the porthole
Into the vast depths beyond

The Realm of Art

Images scrawled with black
Upon snow-white paper
The imperfections of life
Seem so big and yet so small
Amid the white expanse
Of unwritten blank
Not yet yellowed with age
Sitting atop your desk
Like the fog of the future
Representing the world

Write your words down
Let the pen move
Of its own accord
And step into the realm of art
The world of beauty and brittle truth
For art does not lie

Sing your name into
The valleys of serenity
And listen to it echo across the hills
In the shadow of your voice

Take the chance to raise your arms
And fly into the sky on cardboard wings
Feel the sun on your shoulders
Get lost for a time
And feel yourself change

Poems

Poems are a marbled mix of cacophonous emotions
A spell of jumbled words
Spoken with power and intent
One line you catch your breath with joy
Your heart blooming with curiosity
Another line makes you sink to your knees
A torrent of pieces to a thousand puzzles

It is safe to feel the poem
To be confused
To be sad
To be happy
It is okay to cry
To be one with the poem

Touch the paper
Read the words
Piece it together as you smile and sing
Feel with your whole being

You are a poet
Only you can write your own poem

Books Are Candy

Pages upon pages
Of sweet spun tales
Sorrow spun tales
And anger spun tales
Yet all are delicious
Candy words to suck
Until they melt your heart

Some may be lemon
Remembering the hot days
Of summer
Others may be spicy hot
Reminiscent of spite
The bitter taste of revenge
The sweetness of love

Taste them all and write your own
Spin the candy in your hands with bright colors
And choose the flavors carefully

Unwords

Have you ever heard of an unword?
They are like small science experiments
Who were never meant to survive
But somehow did

The defiant little scrap of imagination
That breaks spelling rules
And hides on children's tongues
They tie themselves to the unsuspecting
And the unknowing
And wait for a little slip that allows them
To poke their barbed claws in

Imaginative thinking that breaks society
Perhaps the *architexture* of your apartment building
Is smooth and boring
Perhaps your favorite three-year-old
Has shown you their favorite *ephalant* stuffy
Smiling with joy

So dear serious person
Who believes in exact spelling
And no new unwords
Look around you – you never know
You might find an unword
More *beautimous* than you think

My Stinging Heart

Behind the chain link fence
Red caution tape around her middle
Was my tree

Are those bars made to keep her spirit in
Or my stinging heart out?

Or maybe they are made to keep me from running,
Throwing my arms around her trunk
And pouring my soul over her roots

All her memories now sit against
Pipe and plank and plaster
Smashed and broken on the ground

Waiting for the rain to cry
And soak the damp
Into the cracked foundation

My fingers link through each steel diamond of space
The cold biting through the gloves around my numb hands

Is it strange to grieve the loss of a tree?

She was a living being
Who gave up her life for something new
To emerge from sacred ground

Kepler's Wife

His words they cut like stinging knives
My anger merely a shield
A shield to keep away the pain
But it comes in ever still
A bee's nest full of stinging bees
The honey gone, gone, gone
Forget
Forget
Let go
Let go
Reminding me again, again
My anger starts to grow
My shields are up, again and again
My angry, fiery wall
Get out, get out
You can't come in
But pain comes in again, again
And hurts forever more

Big, Dark, Scary Poem

Searching for something lost and never found
Spinning headfirst into oblivion
A weight so heavy
Pushed under the whirlpool
Hanging on
Hands bloodied
Slipping into unknown
Face first into the ether
Eyes open but no sight
Ears straining but no sound
Silent screaming none can hear
A sopping blanket across your soul
Coating black nothingness
But pain and sickness
Cold as a stare
Yet dry as eating sand
Where are you? Who are you?
What is wrong with you?
Cornered
Slamming through your head
Yelling cruel phrases built by sinister imagination
Tumbling, tripping, flipping kind words
To sarcasm
Round and round and round and round
Damaged and trampled
Gutted and broken
Trapped
Fighting with no return
Regret
Numbness
An abandoned shell
No feeling
Gone forever

It hurts too much to be
The light is impossible
It never was
It never will be

My name is Doubt
And you are my victim

Broken Things

The world will not forget this:

When they carried her, unprotesting
out into the streets
Hair flying
The crazed laughter and keening spilling
Out of the smiling grimace of her face
Her dress like spun sugar

Gather your children! They cried
This girl is a broken thing

Yet, to her, the world was a broken thing
She was a mere shard of it
Waiting
Waiting to come home
Without the blood feuds and the blinding pain

Waiting to change revenge into reverence
And blood into a stain of berries
Never to be washed away

Scars

It's a mistake made
A lesson learned
A battle fought
A victory won
A sign to show you that you can heal
A badge of pain, blood and stamina
A time to show the past
The mark of remembrance
The truth

A time to be proud of your accomplishments
How you tried and got up again
Skinned knees from riding a bike
A cut from using a knife
A scar from the chickenpox

It is a story
A time to show the past
It is the mark of remembrance
It is the truth

Black Dress with Navy Shoes

Who am I to judge you
Based on how your hair looks
Or how you are wearing
Navy shoes with a black dress?

Since when is it my business
To shake my head and imagine
The worst things possible
That come to mind?

Where did we learn to think
Instantly that the conclusion
Will suffice to the fact
That we don't understand it?

How different do you think
Our world would be
If we asked questions before assuming?

How many fights and misunderstandings
Would have been solved
If we began with curiosity instead of fear?

Why does it even matter what we're wearing
Or what we are saying
As we go about our lives?

Maybe they're having a bad day
Or just lost someone close
Or got four hours of sleep?

If we just approached the situation
With compassion instead of resentment
Maybe we would be able to comfort them
And help them have a better day

So if you ever meet someone
Who has red eyes from crying
Or hasn't used a hairbrush for days
Or weeks... or months
Offer kind words
And a grateful smile
And who knows?
Maybe you'll even find a friend

Ode to Joyfulness

Joyfulness
You are a bluebird
Singing for the delight of spring
You are sunny days
Peaceful and calm
With blue skies
And billowy white clouds
You are a rare lavender rose
Blooming up toward the sun
A vibrant yellow
You are laughter
You are pure happiness
You are blue or green or pink or white
You are skipping
Running
And falling
In the green grass

Ode to Grief

Grief, you are a dragon
Wanting to be loved by others
A grey hurricane of emotion
A black thunderstorm of pain
A rainstorm of tears
A sealed box of ashes
Brown and made of wood
A square coffin sealed tight
Never to be opened
Cradling a lost love
Decorated with winding leaf patterns
And the dark stain of tears
Held onto and cried over a million times
Yearning for the one you lost
Grief, you are an oblivion

SMACK!

My friend
You are hurting

The word pain
Could have been written
Across your forehead
In red Sharpie
For, though you try to hide it,
It's unconcealable

You've tripped and you've fallen
Right down those stairs of loss
You're crumpled at the bottom
Head in your hands
You feel beaten and bruised
Slapped, hit and kicked
You're ready to give up

Maybe you start running blindly
Through the hours and the days
But eventually you — SMACK!
Crashed and broken again
You can't go back
To before you said *that*
Or didn't do *this*
You must move forward

But, remember, you can ask for help
Call out or yell, cry or whisper
Someone kind will hear you
They will listen
And will try their hardest
To climb the staircase
Back up with you

Spectrum

Molten colors
Red and gold
Orange bright and yellow bold
Boiling sunset or so I'm told
Hidden treasure in every fold
Of solid rock and pumice cold
Lies the wisdom of centuries old
Of all in nature in reverence hold
Would be volcanoes of another mold
Rumble
Growl
Gurgle
Fuss
Stirring, stirring, stirring

The Hillside of Silent Temples

Forest roots in the sea
Scatter air around each other
Little grains in the sand
Tripping over jump ropes of wind
The silent temples
Their power sparking gold
In the fading sunlight
All the way around
The lush green hillside
Sitting in a cloud

Although the sneaky birds whistle and sing
The fragile leaves still hold strong
For the calmness of winter
Lies beneath the surface
Drowning in beauty

Nightlight

She shines alone
In my arms she carries
Love
Peace
Forgiveness for the world
And light for the people of the skies

Above the waters
She guides the tides with a gentle hand
The earth tide
The air tide
The sea and the sky
They feel not controlled
But one with her

She is the essence of balance
The soft light the sun could never give
The nightlight for the children of millennia
The blanket that allows the strong, weary souls to rest
Waking to survive a new day

Friend of Time

Friend of time
Dream before transforming

When your only wish is laughter,
Believe the blue sky and feel the rain of life

Endure, bless and nourish good

My moment must come from beneath knowing
And where pure light is above hope,
I will play

Luna in Tears

Behind two panes of glass she watches
Her image portrayed not once but thrice
Each more matte than the previous
The glow fading
An old Polaroid camera glitch perhaps
All shaded in black and grey
The moondial pointing ever in one direction
Unswayed by a dark mirage

Do you see the man?
No, I see a girl
Her tears falling from her eyes
Retinas of stone
Her crater of a mouth is open in desperate emotion
Gazing down upon us and our Earth

Charge to the Dark Goddess

Little one
Can you hear my whisper?
How the shadows sing my song?
I am the Queen of Justice
The truth about right and wrong

My eyes are as black as your darkest fear
My skin as white as bone
I move along the midnight hour
And darkness is my home

Child
Can you hear me speaking?
How the shadows praise my name?
Dearest, do not fear me
For I am both the cradle and the grave

The Mind of a Shell

Ask the snail if I was a comfortable home
Ask the seagull if I was a delicious snack
Ask the little boy if I was a delightful toy to play with
And if he cried when he couldn't take me home
Ask the sandy dog if I was fun to roll in
Ask the absentminded human if it was nice to step upon me
Because I have been ground beneath your feet
and built back up
To live the tale:

The truth is they will all sing you a different song

The Ocean

The ocean cries openly
Her tears giving life to the dry sifting sand
The gulls singing in the sky and fighting over crabs
A little girl with a shell clutched in her warm, soft fist
The sandy dogs rolling and chasing the waves
The bottom of the ocean lined with forgotten treasures
Waiting for decades to be found

Invocation to the North

All hail North
The place of Earth
Of plants reaching up toward the sun
Dancing to the music of the wind
The green blades of grass under my feet
The tall brown trunks of the trees
Towering over my head
Of the rolling white hills in winter
And the rich, black soil of fall
Of silent times
The midnight dark
Of the four-legged beasts
And the two-legged gnomes
Bear, squirrel, wolf, deer
The quiet dwellers in pointed hats
Tending with a gentle hand
The mother of giving kindness
Energy flowing through your soul
Into the arms of your grateful children

We welcome thee

Snow

Silent and white
Calm and frozen
Unforgiving in anger
Beautiful in peace
The softest whisper
The swirling storm
Unique in every way
Down to the corner of each flake

Some may jump for joy
At the prospect of snow
Others may sigh in frustration
And some may go about their daily lives
As if nothing has changed

Clear Lake

High in the wooded mountains
Birds sing about stories told
A clear, blue lake
Clear as glass
With trees three thousand years old
Preserved by freezing water
A brilliant turquoise bold
If you tried to touch it
You'd suddenly be cold
The vibrant, sea green lake
Is worth much more than gold

Ode to the Pygmy Owl

Do not judge me by my size
I am small yet I am wise

I silent fly through darkened skies
The mouse I catch my greatest prize

And as you look into my eyes
Somewhere quiet an owl cries

Though I wear this wee disguise
It's a simple trick, a cunning lie

Dragon Eyes

What if felines are but dragons in disguise?
Their hoards
Their territories
Their wings hidden, unseen
They love the high dark places
Like wild, cold stone cliffs
Their irises bright green
Or blue
Or yellow
Or gold
Sleeping
Paws tucked
A loaf of dragon cat
Basking in the noonday sun

One for Kiisa

Pancake-colored, syrup-pawed
A cold, damp chocolate snoot
Pushed under my furless hand
Ears tucked back
Waiting for time and priority
Tail in my face
Chin rubbing against my pen
Tickling my ears with long, white whisker brooms
Little bell jangling
Oozing across my paper or
Kneading into my lap
Circling up in crooks of elbows
Padding onto my chest
To feel the rising waves of breath
Blueberry eyes glowing with a quiet intelligence
Forever my human
Forever my friend

Three-Year-Old Me

After a bath with bubbles
I'm wrapped up
In my ducky towel

I chatter my teeth
Extra loud
Because I like the sound

As I stand there
The cold blue tile sparkles
Merging with the puddles on the floor

Why Home Is Spelled
W-A-L-D-O-R-F

It's all block crayons and colored pencils
Fountain pens and wooden desks
The scent of soup from across the hall
A memory of sheepskin against your cheek

The first grade classroom, inside voices
So as not to wake the sleepy bees
With their resting hum in a cozy glass hive
Lulled by the purr of honey-craft

Glass bottles full of chocolate milk
Yogurt in Ball jars with wooden spoons
The heavy gold bell perched on its homemade cedar stand
Ivy crowns of creekside reeds and unnamed berries red

Rock-Paper-Scissors Tag around the monkey bars
A tree becomes a rocket ship to fly you to the moon
A childhood filled with bubble wrap bishops
Wood scrap boats and cardboard wings

To the Youngest Among Us

Sticky fingers
Reaching up to hold a hand
As you cross the street
Each emotion so simple
Learning the ways of the world
Testing the boundaries
Of other people
And discovering who you are
Little minds ever searching
For any answer you can find
Jumping in puddles
Sliding in mud
Falling in grass
Singing songs out of tune
Clapping games and nursery rhymes
For where imagination merges with reality
No one can tell you what to believe

About the Author

Piper Bringman is a poet and lifelong Waldorf student in Portland, Oregon. She is in 8th grade and spends her days playing soccer, practicing violin, woodworking and learning different kinds of handwork. Outside of school, when she isn't writing poetry, Pi can be found playing piano, snuggling in a beanbag chair with her cats and a fantasy novel, as well as in the ballet studio preparing to perform en pointe in annual renditions of *The Nutcracker*.

Daisy, her German Shepard, is her constant and friendly companion. Together, they watch anime, sketch fashion designs, sing musical scores, eat Thai food and visit with friends. During summer vacations, Piper can be found volunteering at her local humane society as a camp counselor. She loves supporting younger students and being on a first name basis with the shelter pets. Her favorite color is sky blue.

About The Poetry Box®
Young Artist Series

The Poetry Box® was founded by Shawn and Robert Sanders, who wholeheartedly believe that each day spent with the people you love, doing what you love, is a moment in life worth cherishing. Their boutique press celebrates the talents of their fellow artisans and writers through professional book design and the publishing of poetry chapbooks, full-length collections, as well as their flagship journal, The Poeming Pigeon.

With Cardboard Wings, they have launched their Young Artist Series to introduce the next generation of poetic voices in the Portland, Oregon region. The talented young poets in this series are handpicked by acclaimed poet Annie Lighthart, through her work as a poet in the schools. Through this experience, these young writers get their first taste of what it's like to work with an editor and publisher, resulting in a published debut chapbook they can be proud to share.

Feel free to visit the online bookstore (thePoetryBox.com), where you'll find more poetry collections, including recent chapbook prizewinners:

Shrinking Bones by Judy K. Mosher

November Quilt by Penelope Scambly Schott

14: Antologia del Sonoran by Christopher Bogart

Fireweed by Gudrun Bortman

CPSIA information can be obtained
at www.ICGtesting.com
Printed in the USA
BVHW071953210219
540878BV00002B/4/P

9 781948 461276